ZENAB

7 Days of Effective Communication Skills

Unlocking the Power of Oral and Written Communication

First published by Rana Books (UK, INDIA) 2023

Copyright © 2023 by Zenab

All rights reserved. No part of this publication may be reproduced, stored or transmitted in any form or by any means, electronic, mechanical, photocopying, recording, scanning, or otherwise without written permission from the publisher. It is illegal to copy this book, post it to a website, or distribute it by any other means without permission.

First edition

ISBN: 978-81-19786-16-9

Editing by Ranjot Singh Chahal
Cover art by Rana Books UK

Contents

1	Introduction to Effective Communication	1
2	Understanding Oral Communication	6
3	Mastering Written Communication	11
4	Adapting Communication Skills to Different Contexts	18
5	Advanced Communication Skills	23
6	Communication Skills for the Future	31
7	Crisis Communication and Difficult Conversations	40
8	Communication Ethics and Social Responsibility	46
9	Communication in the Digital Age	50
Business English phrases		55
50 Daily life communication tips		59
50 clothing and grooming tips		63
50 oral communication tips		67

1

Introduction to Effective Communication

Effective communication is the process of conveying information or ideas in a clear concise and impactful manner to achieve desired outcomes. It involves both verbal and non-verbal methods to express thoughts opinions and emotions. Effective communication is essential in various aspects of life including personal relationships professional settings and societal interactions.

1.1 Importance of Communication Skills

Communication skills play a vital role in our day-to-day interactions. They are crucial in building and maintaining relationships resolving conflicts understanding others' perspectives and conveying messages effectively. Here are some reasons why communication skills are important:

1.1.1 Building Relationships: Effective communication forms the foundation of strong personal and professional relationships. It allows individuals to connect understand each other and build trust leading to enhanced collaboration and teamwork.

1.1.2 Resolving Conflicts: Miscommunications can often lead to conflicts. By improving communication skills individuals can clarify misunderstandings listen actively express their viewpoints calmly and find mutually acceptable solutions.

1.1.3 Fostering Understanding: Effective communication helps us understand others and their perspectives enabling empathy and a sense of unity. This understanding promotes harmony and reduces misunderstandings and biases.

1.1.4 Enhancing Professional Growth: In professional settings strong communication skills are highly valued. They enable individuals to convey ideas clearly present information convincingly negotiate effectively and engage in successful networking.

1.1.5 Promoting Personal Development: Good communication skills contribute to personal growth and self-confidence. By expressing oneself effectively individuals can assert their needs seek feedback and continuously improve their abilities.

1.2 Benefits of Effective Communication

Developing effective communication skills leads to numerous benefits. Some of these benefits include:

1.2.1 Improved Problem-Solving: Effective communication helps in identifying and understanding problems accurately. It enables individuals to exchange information seek different perspectives and collaboratively find appropriate solutions.

1.2.2 Increased Productivity: Clear communication eliminates confusion and ensures that tasks are understood correctly. This leads to improved efficiency reduced errors and overall increased productivity.

1.2.3 Enhanced Professional Image: Individuals with strong communication skills are more likely to be seen as competent credible and reliable. They are perceived as better leaders collaborators and team members which can lead to greater career opportunities.

1.2.4 Better Work Relationships: Effective communication fosters positive relationships in the workplace. It allows for clearer instructions active listening and constructive feedback creating a supportive and harmonious work environment.

1.2.5 Improved Customer Relations: Good communication skills contribute to satisfying customer experiences. It enables effective listening to customer needs addressing concerns promptly and delivering clear instructions or explanations.

1.3 Overview of Oral and Written Communication

Effective communication can be achieved through both oral and written methods. Each has its advantages and is suited for different contexts. Here is a brief overview of these communication modes:

1.3.1 Oral Communication: Oral communication refers to the

exchange of information through spoken words and includes face-to-face conversations meetings presentations and phone calls. It allows for immediate feedback clarification and non-verbal cues like body language and tone of voice making it a dynamic form of communication. Oral communication is often preferred for interactive discussions negotiations and situations that require real-time interaction.

Example 1: In a business meeting oral communication is crucial for colleagues to discuss brainstorm ideas and reach mutual decisions. The interactive nature of oral communication allows participants to ask questions clarify doubts and engage in active dialogue.

Example 2: In a customer service scenario oral communication is valuable as it enables service representatives to listen actively to customer concerns provide immediate responses and offer personalized solutions. The ability to convey empathy and understanding through tone of voice contributes to a positive customer experience.

1.3.2 Written Communication: Written communication involves the use of written or printed words to convey messages. It includes emails reports memos letters social media posts and other written forms. Written communication provides a permanent record of information and allows recipients to review and refer back to the message. It is often used for conveying complex information formal communication and reaching a larger audience.

Example 1: In an organization written communication is essential for sharing important information with employees. For instance an email announcing a company-wide policy change ensures that all employees receive consistent and precise information that they can refer to as needed.

Example 2: Written communication is crucial in academic settings. Research papers essays and assignments allow students to convey their understanding of a subject in a structured and coherent manner. Written communication in this context enables students to present logical arguments support their claims with evidence and showcase their writing skills.

In conclusion effective communication skills are vital for personal professional and societal interactions. They facilitate building relationships resolving conflicts fostering understanding and promoting personal and professional growth. Effective communication can be achieved through various modes including oral and written communication each suited for different contexts. By developing these skills individuals can enhance their problem-solving capabilities productivity professional image work relationships and customer relations.

2

Understanding Oral Communication

2.1 Elements of Effective Oral Communication

Oral communication is the process of conveying information or messages through spoken words. To ensure effective oral communication it is important to understand and utilize various elements such as verbal communication nonverbal communication and listening skills.

2.1.1 Verbal Communication: Words and Language

Verbal communication is the use of words and language to convey information. It involves choosing the right words sentence structure and tone to express ideas clearly and effectively. For example when giving a presentation using concise and well-organized language helps the audience understand the message easily.

Example: In a business meeting a team leader effectively communicates the goals and objectives of a project by using clear and specific language highlighting key points and addressing any potential misunderstandings.

2.1.2 Nonverbal Communication: Body Language Gestures and Facial Expressions

Nonverbal communication refers to the use of body language gestures and facial expressions to convey information and emotions. It plays an important role in enhancing the clarity and impact of oral communication. For instance maintaining eye contact using appropriate hand gestures and displaying facial expressions that align with the message can help reinforce the intended meaning.

Example: While delivering a speech a confident speaker uses hand gestures and facial expressions to engage the audience demonstrating enthusiasm and conviction about the topic being discussed.

2.1.3 Listening Skills: Active Listening and Reflective Listening

Effective oral communication also requires good listening skills. Active listening involves paying close attention to the speaker understanding the message being conveyed and providing appropriate verbal or nonverbal responses. Reflective listening involves paraphrasing or summarizing what the speaker said to clarify understanding and show empathy.

Example: During a team discussion an attentive listener actively engages in the conversation by nodding maintaining eye contact and asking relevant questions to ensure a clear understanding of the speaker's perspective.

2.2 Barriers to Effective Oral Communication

There are various barriers that can hinder effective oral communication. It is important to identify and address these barriers to ensure effective communication.

2.2.1 Psychological Barriers: Attitudes and Perceptions

Psychological barriers arise from personal attitudes beliefs and perceptions that can impact communication. Preconceived notions biases and defensive attitudes can hinder understanding and create misunderstandings.

Example: In a multicultural workplace different cultural backgrounds may lead to misunderstandings and misinterpretations if individuals do not actively work to understand and appreciate each other's perspectives.

2.2.2 Language Barriers: Jargon and Technical Language

Language barriers occur when there is a mismatch in language proficiency or when technical jargon is used making it difficult for others to understand. This can create confusion and hinder effective communication.

Example: In a medical setting doctors communicating with patients need to use plain and simple language to ensure patients understand their medical condition and prescribed treatments.

2.2.3 Environmental Barriers: Noise and Distractions

Environmental barriers can disrupt effective oral communication. Background noise interruptions or distractions in the environment can make it difficult to hear or concentrate on the message being conveyed.

Example: During an important conference call noise from construction outside the office may hinder effective communication requiring participants to find a quieter location or use headphones to minimize distractions.

2.3 Developing Effective Oral Communication Skills

Developing effective oral communication skills is essential for conveying messages clearly and achieving effective understanding. Here are some key skills to focus on:

2.3.1 Clear and Concise Speech

Clear and concise speech involves articulating thoughts clearly using appropriate language avoiding unnecessary jargon or technical terms and structuring the message in a logical and coherent manner.

Example: In a customer service role a representative ensures clear and concise speech by avoiding complex technical terms using simple language and providing relevant and concise explanations to address customer queries effectively.

2.3.2 Effective Presentation and Public Speaking Techniques

Presentation and public speaking techniques involve using visual aids structuring the speech maintaining eye contact with the audience using appropriate gestures and employing vocal variations to engage the audience effectively.

Example: During a business presentation a sales manager effectively engages the audience by using visual slides maintaining eye contact speaking clearly and confidently and using appropriate body language to emphasize key points.

2.3.3 Building Rapport and Active Engagement

Building rapport and active engagement involves creating a positive and interactive environment to foster effective communication. This includes active listening asking questions providing feedback and showing empathy.

Example: In a counseling session a therapist builds rapport and active engagement by actively listening to the client's concerns asking open-ended questions reflecting on the client's emotions and providing empathetic responses.

In conclusion understanding the elements of effective oral communication recognizing barriers and developing essential skills can greatly enhance one's ability to convey messages clearly build rapport and engage listeners effectively.

3

Mastering Written Communication

In today's digital age effective written communication is crucial for success in both personal and professional settings. Whether it's writing emails crafting reports or communicating through social media being able to express yourself clearly and concisely is essential. This section will delve into the principles of effective written communication strategies for overcoming challenges and techniques for enhancing your written communication skills.

3.1 Principles of Effective Written Communication

To communicate effectively in writing there are several key principles you should keep in mind:

3.1.1 Clarity: Structure Grammar and Punctuation

One of the most important aspects of written communication is clarity. Your message should be structured in a logical and organized manner so that readers can easily understand your intentions. Start with a clear introduction develop your arguments or ideas in the body of the text and conclude with a concise summary or call-to-action. Each paragraph should focus on one main idea and be connected through transitional phrases.

Grammar and punctuation play a vital role in conveying your message accurately. Proper sentence construction correct verb tenses subject-verb agreement and the appropriate use of punctuation marks are all essential in ensuring clarity. For example consider the difference between "Let's eat Grandma!" and "Let's eat Grandma!" The placement of a simple comma changes the entire meaning of the sentence.

3.1.2 Brevity: Concise and to-the-point Writing

In today's fast-paced world brevity is valued. A concise and to-the-point writing style not only saves time for both the writer and the reader but it also enhances clarity. Avoid using unnecessary words phrases or jargon that may confuse or bore your audience. Instead focus on delivering your message using simple and precise language.

For instance compare these two sentences: "In my opinion I believe that we should consider implementing a more sustainable approach to waste management" and "We should adopt a sustainable approach to waste management." The second sentence conveys the same message in a more concise and direct manner.

3.1.3 Tone and Style: Adaptability and Professionalism

The tone and style of your writing play a significant role in how your message is perceived. Different situations require different tones whether it's formal informal professional or casual. Consider your audience and adjust your tone accordingly.

Professionalism is key when it comes to business communication. Avoid using slang colloquialisms or overly personal language. Use a formal and respectful tone and tailor your writing style to align with the expectations of your organization or industry.

For example compare the tone and style of an email to a friend versus an email to a senior executive. In the former you might use a more casual tone whereas in the latter a formal and respectful tone would be more appropriate.

3.2 Overcoming Challenges in Written Communication

Even the most skilled writers face challenges when it comes to written communication. Here are some common challenges and strategies for overcoming them:

3.2.1 Avoiding Ambiguity and Misinterpretation

Ambiguity in writing can lead to confusion and misunderstandings. To avoid this ensure your message is clear concise and free from vague language. Use specific words and provide examples or evidence to support your ideas. Always read your writing from the perspective of the reader to identify any potential areas of ambiguity.

Additionally consider the cultural and linguistic backgrounds of your readers. Be conscious of potential language barriers and strive to communicate in a way that transcends these barriers. If necessary provide explanations or definitions of key terms or cultural references.

3.2.2 Overcoming Writer's Block and Procrastination

Writer's block and procrastination are common hurdles that can impede your ability to communicate effectively in writing. To overcome writer's block try different strategies such as brainstorming outlining or freewriting. Taking breaks seeking inspiration from other sources or discussing ideas with others can also help overcome mental blocks.

Procrastination on the other hand can be dealt with by breaking your writing tasks into smaller manageable chunks. Establishing a realistic timeline setting deadlines and creating a conducive writing environment can help you stay focused and motivated.

3.2.3 Proofreading and Editing Techniques

To ensure the accuracy and professionalism of your written communication you need to dedicate time and effort to proofreading and editing your work. Proofreading involves checking for spelling grammar punctuation and formatting errors while editing focuses on overall coherence and clarity.

Develop a systematic approach to proofreading and editing. Start by reviewing your work for basic errors such as spelling and grammar mistakes. Then focus on the structure and organization of your writing ensuring that each paragraph flows logically and supports your main points. Finally read your work aloud to catch any awkward phrasing or unclear sentences.

3.3 Enhancing Written Communication Skills

To enhance your written communication skills it's essential to focus on specific types of written communication commonly used in various settings. Here are three areas to consider:

3.3.1 Writing Effective Emails and Memos

Emails and memos are widely used for communication in the workplace. To write effective emails start with a clear subject line that summarizes the purpose of your message. Keep your content concise use proper greetings and salutations and address recipients directly. Use clear headings and bullet points to organize information and always proofread before sending.

Memos on the other hand are more formal and typically used for internal communication within organizations. Memos should have a clear purpose be structured with headings and subsections and present information in a concise and easily understandable manner. Avoid using overly technical jargon and jargon specific to your organization and remember to use a professional and respectful tone.

3.3.2 Crafting Clear and Persuasive Reports

Reports are important tools for conveying information and

making informed decisions. A well-crafted report should have a clear structure including an executive summary introduction body and conclusion. Use headings and subheadings to organize your content and provide relevant data evidence and examples to support your findings.

To make your report persuasive consider your audience's needs and interests. Tailor your arguments and recommendations to resonate with your readers. Use persuasive language and provide strong evidence to support your claims. Lastly make sure your report is visually appealing by incorporating graphs charts and tables to present data effectively.

3.3.3 Communicating in a Digital Age: Social Media and Online Platforms

In today's digital age social media and online platforms play a significant role in written communication. Whether it's personal or professional communication it's crucial to adapt your writing style to suit these platforms.

When communicating through social media be mindful of your audience and the platform's specific requirements. Use concise and attention-grabbing language hashtags and visuals to enhance engagement. Remember to proofread your posts to avoid errors as they can quickly spread on social media.

When participating in online platforms such as forums or discussion boards maintain a respectful and professional tone. Clearly articulate your thoughts and ideas and provide meaningful contributions to ongoing discussions. Avoid confrontational language and engage in constructive dialogue.

In conclusion mastering written communication is essential in today's world. By following the principles of clarity brevity and adapting your tone and style to the situation you can effectively convey your message. Overcoming challenges such as ambiguity writer's block and procrastination requires practice and perseverance. Finally enhancing your skills in specific areas such as writing emails crafting reports and using online platforms will further strengthen your written communication abilities.

4

Adapting Communication Skills to Different Contexts

Communication is a fundamental aspect of human interaction and effective communication skills are essential in navigating different contexts. Adapting one's communication style and approach to suit the specific circumstances is key to building strong relationships thriving in the workplace and embracing diversity. In this section we will delve into three specific contexts: interpersonal communication professional communication and cross-cultural communication. We will explore the skills necessary for each context and provide examples to illustrate their importance.

4.1 Interpersonal Communication: Building Strong Relationships

Interpersonal communication refers to the exchange of information feelings and meaning between individuals. It plays a crucial role in building and maintaining relationships whether personal or professional. Here are two important skills within the framework of interpersonal communication:

4.1.1 Active Listening and Empathy

Active listening involves attentively openly and non-judgmentally receiving and understanding the speaker's message. It requires focusing not only on the words being said but also on the speaker's tone body language and emotional cues. Active listening fosters a sense of understanding and validation. By actively listening one can demonstrate empathy which is the ability to understand and share the feelings of others.

For example let's say a friend is going through a difficult time. Instead of simply providing advice or solutions active listening involves giving them your full attention suspending judgment and empathizing with their emotions. By doing so you create a safe space for them to express themselves and feel understood.

4.1.2 Conflict Resolution and Negotiation

Conflict resolution and negotiation skills are vital when differences arise in relationships. It is inevitable for conflicts to occur from time to time and the ability to resolve these conflicts in a constructive way is essential for maintaining healthy interactions.

For instance in a professional setting two colleagues may have differing opinions regarding a project. Conflict resolution skills involve actively seeking common ground using effective communication techniques to address concerns and collaborating to reach a mutually beneficial solution. By finding compromises and engaging in open dialogue conflicts can be resolved without damaging the relationship or impeding progress.

4.2 Professional Communication: Thriving in the Workplace

In the workplace effective communication is crucial for productivity teamwork and professional growth. Here are two key skills within professional communication:

4.2.1 Effective Team Communication

Collaboration within teams requires effective communication to ensure that everyone is aligned informed and working towards shared goals. This involves concise and clear communication active listening and providing and receiving constructive feedback.

For example during a team meeting effective communication involves actively engaging in discussions ensuring that everyone's input is heard and respected and sharing relevant information. By doing so team members can work together efficiently and build strong working relationships.

4.2.2 Presenting Ideas and Proposals

Presenting ideas and proposals is common in professional settings whether it's in meetings conferences or project pitches. The ability to articulate thoughts clearly engage the audience and convey information persuasively is critical.

For instance during a business presentation effective communication involves structuring the content in a logical manner using visual aids to support key points and delivering the information with confidence and enthusiasm. By doing so the audience can better understand and appreciate the ideas being presented.

4.3 Cross-Cultural Communication: Embracing Diversity

In today's interconnected world cross-cultural communication skills are essential for interacting with individuals from different cultural backgrounds. It involves understanding and respecting different cultural norms values and communication styles. Here are two important skills within cross-cultural communication:

4.3.1 Cultural Awareness and Sensitivity

Cultural awareness refers to having knowledge and understanding of different cultures including their customs traditions and non-verbal cues. Sensitivity to cultural differences is the ability to recognize and respect these differences when interacting with individuals from diverse cultural backgrounds.

For example in a multicultural team cultural awareness and sensitivity involve recognizing that diverse perspectives and approaches are valuable. It also means being mindful of potential misunderstandings that may arise due to cultural differences and proactively seeking clarification when needed.

4.3.2 Overcoming Language and Cultural Barriers

When communicating across language and cultural barriers it is important to adapt one's communication style to ensure effective understanding. This may involve using simpler language avoiding idioms or slang and being mindful of non-verbal cues.

For instance if you are conducting a business negotiation with individuals from a different cultural background it is crucial to anticipate language and cultural barriers. Adapting communication by using clear and simple language providing visual aids and being patient and understanding can help facilitate effective communication and bridge any gaps.

In conclusion adapting communication skills to different contexts is essential for building strong relationships thriving in the workplace and embracing diversity. Active listening and empathy foster understanding in interpersonal communication while conflict resolution and negotiation skills help in resolving conflicts constructively. Effective team communication and presenting ideas and proposals are vital in professional settings. Lastly cultural awareness sensitivity and overcoming language and cultural barriers are crucial in cross-cultural communication. By developing and applying these skills individuals can navigate various contexts successfully and promote effective communication.

5

Advanced Communication Skills

Effective communication is essential in all aspects of life whether it's personal relationships professional settings or even casual interactions. Advanced communication skills go beyond just conveying information and actively foster understanding empathy and persuasion. In this section we will explore two important aspects of advanced communication skills: emotional intelligence in communication and persuasive communication techniques. Additionally we'll discuss leading effective conversations and meetings focusing on facilitation techniques and managing feedback and conflict.

5.1 Emotional Intelligence in Communication

Emotional intelligence (EI) refers to the ability to understand and manage your own emotions and the emotions of others. It plays a crucial role in communication as it enables individuals to express themselves effectively empathize with others and navigate conflicts more constructively.

5.1.1 Self-awareness and Self-regulation

Self-awareness is the foundation of emotional intelligence. It involves understanding your emotions preferences strengths and weaknesses. By cultivating self-awareness you can better understand how your emotions influence your communication and make conscious choices to regulate your responses.

For example imagine you're in a team meeting discussing a project. By being self-aware and recognizing that you tend to become defensive when your ideas are challenged you can consciously regulate your reactions and respond more constructively. Instead of getting defensive you can actively listen to others' viewpoints and find common ground.

Self-regulation also involves managing your emotional state. Practicing techniques such as deep breathing mindfulness or taking a brief pause before responding can help you maintain composure especially in emotionally charged situations and communicate more effectively.

5.1.2 Building Empathy and Emotional Connections

Empathy is the ability to understand and share the feelings of others. It's a crucial skill for building meaningful connections and fostering effective communication. When you demonstrate empathy you show genuine interest listen actively and validate others' emotions.

For example imagine your colleague is having a rough day and seems upset. Instead of ignoring or dismissing their emotions you can take a moment to empathize. You can say something like "I can see that you're feeling down. Is there anything I can do to help or support you?"

By actively listening and acknowledging their emotions you establish a connection and create a safe space for open communication. This kind of empathetic response fosters trust and strengthens relationships making it more likely that your colleague will open up and share their concerns or thoughts.

Empathy can also help navigate conflicts. By putting yourself in the other person's shoes you can better understand their perspective and find mutually agreeable solutions. This approach allows for more constructive communication and reduces the chances of misunderstandings or escalating conflicts.

5.2 Persuasive Communication Techniques

Persuasive communication involves the ability to influence others' beliefs attitudes and behaviors. Whether you're trying to convince someone to adopt a certain viewpoint support a project or make a purchase persuasive communication techniques can help you present your ideas effectively and increase your chances of success.

5.2.1 Building a Compelling Argument

To build a compelling argument it's important to structure your communication effectively provide evidence and reasoning to support your claims and engage your audience. Here are some key techniques to enhance your persuasive communication skills:

- Clearly Define the Purpose: Clearly state your goal and what you want to achieve through your communication. This will help you stay focused and ensure your message is coherent.

- Understand Your Audience: Tailor your communication to your audience's needs interests and values. Consider what is important to them and the potential objections they might have. By addressing these concerns you increase the chances of persuading them.

- Use Logic and Reasoning: Present your ideas logically and provide supporting evidence. Use facts research findings examples and expert opinions to strengthen your argument. This helps your audience see the validity and credibility of your viewpoint.

- Appeal to Emotions: Emotions can play a powerful role in persuasion. Use storytelling metaphors and vivid language to evoke emotions and create a connection with your audience. However be mindful of ethical considerations and avoid manipulating emotions for unethical purposes.

- Anticipate and Address Counterarguments: Acknowledge potential counterarguments and address them directly. By recognizing and responding to opposing viewpoints you demonstrate thoughtfulness and credibility. This also helps to build trust and shows that you have considered different perspectives.

- Call to Action: Clearly articulate what action or decision you want your audience to take. Make it easy for them to understand how they can benefit from your proposal and provide clear instructions on what they should do next.

5.2.2 Influencing and Negotiation Skills

Influencing and negotiation skills are essential for achieving desired outcomes resolving conflicts and building mutually beneficial relationships. These skills involve understanding others' perspectives and needs finding common ground and working towards win-win solutions.

- Active Listening: Actively listen to understand the other person's viewpoint needs and concerns. By demonstrating that you value their input you can build rapport and create a foundation for effective negotiation.

- Finding Common Ground: Identify shared goals or interests that both parties can agree on. Highlighting these commonalities helps create a cooperative atmosphere and encourages collaboration.

- Win-Win Solutions: Look for solutions that meet the needs and interests of all parties involved. By finding mutually beneficial outcomes you increase the chances of reaching an agreement and maintaining positive relationships.

- Effective Communication: Use clear and concise language to express your thoughts needs and priorities. Be open to feedback and ask clarifying questions to ensure understanding. Avoid confrontational language or tactics that may escalate conflicts.

- Compromise and Flexibility: Be willing to compromise and find middle-ground solutions. Successful negotiation often requires flexibility and the ability to let go of some demands in favor of achieving a mutually acceptable outcome.

5.3 Leading Effective Conversations and Meetings

Leading conversations and meetings involves facilitating effective communication managing conflicts and ensuring that everyone's perspectives are heard. By employing specific techniques you can create an inclusive and productive environment for discussions and decision-making.

5.3.1 Facilitation Techniques

- Setting Clear Objectives: Clearly define the purpose and objectives of the conversation or meeting. This helps participants stay focused and understand what they need to accomplish.

- Active Listening and Encouraging Participation: Encourage active participation by making it clear that everyone's perspectives are valued. Actively listen to each participant and ensure that everyone has an opportunity to share their thoughts.

- Maintaining a Constructive Atmosphere: Set ground rules to create a respectful environment where everyone feels comfortable expressing their opinions. Address any disruptive behaviors or conflicts that may arise and redirect the conversation back to its purpose.

- Summarizing and Synthesizing Information: Regularly summarize key points and clarify any ambiguities or misunderstandings. This helps participants stay engaged and ensures that everyone is on the same page.

- Time Management: Manage the conversation or meeting's time effectively by setting time limits for each agenda item. Be mindful of the group's energy and attention span and adjust the pace accordingly.

5.3.2 Managing Feedback and Conflict

- Encourage Constructive Feedback: Create an atmosphere where feedback is encouraged and seen as an opportunity for growth. Provide specific feedback that focuses on the behavior or action rather than personal attacks.

- Addressing Conflict: When conflicts arise remain calm and impartial. Act as a mediator facilitating an open and respectful dialogue between the parties involved. Encourage active listening empathy and finding common ground.

- Finding Mutually Acceptable Solutions: Help the parties involved identify shared interests and work towards mutually acceptable solutions. Encourage compromise and ensure that everyone's needs and concerns are addressed.

Conclusion:

Advanced communication skills are vital for personal and professional success. Developing emotional intelligence in communication allows individuals to better understand themselves and others build empathy and navigate conflicts more effectively. Furthermore persuasive communication techniques enable individuals to present information effectively influence others' beliefs and behaviors and negotiate win-win solutions. Leading effective conversations and meetings involves facilitating communication managing conflicts and ensuring inclusivity and productivity. By mastering these advanced communication skills individuals can enhance their relationships achieve desired outcomes and contribute to positive and effective communication environments.

6

Communication Skills for the Future

In the ever-changing digital landscape effective communication skills are becoming increasingly important. As technology continues to evolve new communication trends and innovations are emerging and individuals must adapt to stay relevant in their personal and professional lives. This section explores some of the key communication skills needed for the future and how individuals can develop and improve upon them.

6.1 Digital Communication Trends and Innovations

6.1.1 Virtual Communication: Video Conferencing and Remote Collaboration

Virtual communication has become a prominent part of our lives especially with the rise of remote work. Video conferencing tools like Zoom Microsoft Teams and Google Meet have become essential for connecting with colleagues clients and teams across the globe. Being able to effectively communicate through virtual platforms is a crucial skill for the future.

To excel in virtual communication it is essential to learn how to make eye contact by looking directly at the camera as it creates a sense of connection with the person on the other end. Additionally using body language effectively even through a screen can help convey your message more clearly. Being mindful of your surroundings and having an organized and well-prepared presentation can also make a significant impact on your virtual communication skills.

Furthermore active listening is crucial during virtual interactions. It involves giving your full attention to the person speaking avoiding interruptions and summarizing or paraphrasing what they said to ensure understanding. By actively listening and engaging in virtual conversations you can build stronger relationships and create a more collaborative and productive remote work environment.

6.1.2 Artificial Intelligence and Natural Language Processing

Artificial Intelligence (AI) and Natural Language Processing (NLP) are revolutionizing the way we communicate. AI-powered technologies such as voice assistants and chatbots are already being integrated into our daily lives. These technologies are capable of understanding human language and responding with meaningful and context-specific information.

To effectively communicate with AI and utilize NLP technology individuals need to develop skills such as clarity specificity and brevity. AI systems often rely on data inputs and algorithms to provide information and responses. As such clear and concise communication is necessary to ensure accurate and relevant outcomes.

Moreover individuals should be adept at asking the right questions and providing relevant information to AI systems. Understanding the limitations and capabilities of AI is crucial to achieving desired results. By learning how to harness the power of AI and NLP individuals can enhance their communication skills and maximize their productivity and efficiency.

6.2 Lifelong Learning and Improving Communication Skills

6.2.1 Personal Development Strategies

Improving communication skills is a continuous process that requires ongoing personal development. Here are some strategies to enhance your communication skills for the future:

a. Seek feedback: Actively seek feedback from peers mentors or supervisors. Ask for specific areas of improvement and work on enhancing those aspects of your communication.

b. Practice active listening: Engage in active listening exercises to improve your listening skills. Focus on understanding others' perspectives thoughts and emotions and practice summarizing or paraphrasing their points to demonstrate your comprehension.

c. Enhance non-verbal communication: Non-verbal communication including body language facial expressions and tone of voice plays a vital role in effective communication. Pay attention to your non-verbal cues and practice being mindful of how they affect your message.

d. Embrace cultural diversity: In today's globalized world it is essential to be aware of and sensitive to cultural differences. Learn about different cultural communication styles and norms as this knowledge will help you navigate cross-cultural communications more successfully.

e. Develop empathy: Empathy is the ability to understand and share the feelings of others. Cultivating empathy allows you to connect with people on a deeper level facilitating more meaningful and effective communication.

f. Use storytelling: Storytelling is an effective communication tool that can captivate your audience and help convey your message more memorably. Learn storytelling techniques and incorporate them into your presentations and conversations.

6.2.2 Continuous Improvement and Growth Mindset

To thrive in the future it is essential to adopt a growth mindset and continuously seek opportunities for improvement. Here are some strategies to embrace continuous improvement in communication skills:

a. Embrace challenges: View communication challenges as opportunities for growth. Embrace difficult conversations and situations as chances to hone your communication skills and learn from them.

b. Reflect on past interactions: Regularly reflect on your past communication experiences. Identify areas where you excelled and areas where you can improve. Consider the impact of your communication on others and adjust your approach as needed.

c. Set specific goals: Establish specific communication goals to work towards. These goals can be related to areas such as public speaking conflict resolution or communication in specific contexts (e.g virtual communication). Break down these goals into smaller manageable steps to track your progress.

d. Seek learning opportunities: Attend workshops seminars or online courses that focus on communication skills development. Stay updated on emerging trends and research in the field of communication to continually expand your knowledge.

e. Practice practice practice: Actively seek opportunities to practice your communication skills. Engage in conversations debates or public speaking events to refine your abilities. Practice with friends family or colleagues and ask for constructive feedback to enhance your skills.

f. Stay curious: Stay curious and open-minded to new ideas perspectives and communication styles. Engaging in diverse conversations and seeking out different viewpoints can expand your communication repertoire and make you a more effective communicator.

In conclusion effective communication skills are essential for personal and professional success both now and in the future. As technology advances it is crucial to adapt to digital communication trends and innovations such as virtual communication and AI-driven interactions. Additionally lifelong learning and a growth mindset are integral to improving communication skills continually. By embracing personal development strategies and seeking opportunities for improvement individuals can elevate their communication skills and thrive in an ever-evolving world.

50 tips for communication skills that will help individuals navigate the challenges and opportunities of the future:

1. Embrace Technology: Stay updated with the latest communication tools and platforms.
2. Practice Active Listening: Pay full attention when others speak.
3. Develop Empathy: Understand and relate to others' perspectives.
4. Improve Nonverbal Communication: Be aware of your body language and facial expressions.
5. Adapt Your Communication Style: Tailor your message to your audience.
6. Be Clear and Concise: Avoid unnecessary jargon or complexity.
7. Enhance Digital Literacy: Understand online communication trends and tools.
8. Emphasize Emotional Intelligence: Recognize and manage your emotions.
9. Use Visual Aids: Incorporate visuals to enhance your message.
10. Master the Art of Storytelling: Craft compelling narratives.
11. Cultivate Cultural Sensitivity: Respect diverse cultural norms.

12. Develop Conflict Resolution Skills: Address disagreements constructively.
13. Build a Personal Brand: Maintain a consistent online presence.
14. Prioritize Data Privacy: Protect personal and sensitive information.
15. Learn from Feedback: Welcome criticism as an opportunity for growth.
16. Be Mindful of Tone: Choose words and phrases carefully.
17. Foster Collaboration: Encourage teamwork and shared communication.
18. Practice Public Speaking: Hone your presentation skills.
19. Engage in Active Networking: Build professional relationships.
20. Leverage AI Tools: Use AI-driven insights for communication improvement.
21. Stay Informed: Be aware of global events and trends.
22. Be Adaptable: Adjust your communication style as situations change.
23. Develop Crisis Communication Plans: Prepare for unforeseen challenges.
24. Foster Inclusivity: Ensure all voices are heard in discussions.
25. Use Social Media Strategically: Share valuable content and engage with your audience.
26. Implement Video Conferencing Etiquette: Look and sound professional on video calls.
27. Enhance Email Etiquette: Write clear, concise, and polite emails.
28. Collaborate Across Time Zones: Coordinate with colleagues in different locations.

29. Be Open to New Ideas: Encourage innovation and creativity in discussions.
30. Mind Your Online Reputation: Monitor and manage your digital footprint.
31. Understand AI Communication Tools: Leverage chatbots and automated responses.
32. Promote Ethical Communication: Uphold honesty and integrity in all interactions.
33. Develop Crisis Communication Skills: Respond effectively in high-pressure situations.
34. Master Data Visualization: Present complex information in an understandable way.
35. Learn a Second Language: Facilitate communication with diverse groups.
36. Stay Organized: Manage communication channels and information effectively.
37. Use Social Listening Tools: Monitor online conversations about your brand.
38. Cultivate Resilience: Bounce back from communication setbacks.
39. Hone Negotiation Skills: Reach mutually beneficial agreements.
40. Foster Transparency: Share information openly with stakeholders.
41. Seek Mentorship: Learn from experienced communicators.
42. Avoid Information Overload: Prioritize and filter information.
43. Develop a Crisis Communication Team: Assign roles and responsibilities.
44. Monitor AI Ethics: Ensure AI-driven communication aligns with ethical standards.

45. Understand User Experience (UX): Tailor communication for a positive experience.
46. Enhance Data Security Awareness: Protect against cyber threats.
47. Embrace Sustainable Practices: Communicate your commitment to sustainability.
48. Stay Current with Communication Research: Incorporate best practices.
49. Practice Mindfulness: Reduce stress and enhance focus in communication.
50. Foster Lifelong Learning: Continuously improve your communication skills.

7

Crisis Communication and Difficult Conversations

In any organization or personal setting crisis situations and difficult conversations are bound to arise at some point. These situations can be challenging emotional and potentially detrimental to relationships and reputation if not handled effectively. Therefore it is crucial to have strategies in place to navigate these conversations with care and professionalism. This section will provide insights on crisis communication and offer guidance on how to manage difficult conversations.

7.1 Strategies for Handling Crisis Communication

Crisis communication refers to the process of conveying information during an unexpected event or situation that can potentially damage an individual's or organization's reputation. In these situations it is important to act swiftly thoughtfully and transparently to mitigate the impact of the crisis. Here are some strategies to consider:

7.1.1 Crisis Response Plans and Preparedness

One effective way to handle crisis communication is to develop a crisis response plan in advance. This plan outlines the steps to be taken in the event of a crisis including designated spokespersons communication channels and procedures for gathering and disseminating information. By having a well-prepared plan the organization can respond promptly efficiently and with consistency.

For example consider a company that experiences a security breach resulting in the compromise of customer data. Without a crisis response plan the organization might scramble to respond causing confusion and eroding trust. However with a prepared plan they can proactively communicate the breach inform affected clients and take appropriate measures to rectify the situation.

7.1.2 Communicating with Empathy during Crisis

During a crisis people are often emotionally affected and may feel vulnerable or anxious. It is crucial to communicate with empathy and understanding to establish trust and support. Here are some key points to consider:

- Acknowledge emotions: Recognize and validate the emotions of those affected by the crisis. This can be done by expressing empathy and understanding for their concerns or frustrations.

- Provide transparent information: Be open and honest about the situation sharing relevant information to the best of your knowledge. This allows individuals to make informed decisions and reduces the likelihood of misinformation or panic.

- Offer support and resources: Provide assistance and resources to those affected such as helplines counseling services or alternative solutions. This demonstrates your commitment to resolving the crisis and helping individuals navigate through it.

For instance in a healthcare organization if there is a medication recall due to safety concerns communicating with empathy is crucial. The organization should acknowledge the impact on patients and caregivers provide clear instructions on next steps and offer support resources to address any concerns or questions.

7.2 Navigating Difficult Conversations

Difficult conversations can occur in various personal and professional contexts. These conversations may involve conflict disagreements or addressing sensitive topics. It is essential to approach these conversations tactfully and constructively to achieve positive outcomes and maintain healthy relationships. Here are some strategies for navigating difficult conversations:

7.2.1 Dealing with Conflict and Disagreements

Conflicts and disagreements are a natural part of human interaction. However by approaching them with a calm and solution-oriented mindset it is possible to resolve issues effectively. Consider the following techniques:

- Active listening: Pay attention to the other person's perspective ideas and concerns. Demonstrate respect and empathy by giving them your full attention maintaining eye contact and avoiding interrupting. Reflect back their key points to ensure you understand their viewpoint.

- Focus on interests not positions: Instead of getting stuck on opposing positions try to identify the underlying interests and needs of all parties involved. This helps find common ground and explore mutually beneficial solutions.

- Collaborative problem-solving: Encourage a collaborative approach to problem-solving by inviting input from all parties involved. Brainstorm potential solutions together evaluate their pros and cons and strive for a compromise that is agreeable to everyone.

For instance imagine a team at work that is experiencing conflicts around project deadlines. By actively listening to each team member's concerns identifying common goals and finding solutions that accommodate everyone's needs the team can address the conflicts and improve collaboration.

7.2.2 Providing Constructive Feedback

Providing feedback is an essential part of personal and professional growth. However delivering feedback in a constructive and respectful manner is crucial to avoid damaging relationships or discouraging individuals. Here are some tips for providing effective feedback:

- Be specific and objective: Clearly identify the behavior or actions that require feedback. Focus on observable facts rather than personal opinions or assumptions. This helps maintain an objective approach and reduces defensiveness.

- Use the "sandwich" approach: Start and end the feedback session with positive and constructive feedback sandwiching the areas of improvement in between. This balanced approach helps maintain motivation and facilitates open communication.

- Offer suggestions and solutions: Instead of simply pointing out problems provide guidance and suggestions for improvement. Offer actionable steps or resources that can help the individual develop and grow.

For example if you are a supervisor providing feedback to an employee who consistently misses deadlines you can start by acknowledging their strengths and contributions then address the issue by offering guidance on time management techniques or providing additional resources and support.

7.2.3 Addressing Sensitive Topics

Sensitive topics can be challenging to discuss as they often involve personal beliefs cultural differences or emotional aspects. However addressing these topics respectfully and constructively is crucial for fostering understanding and promoting inclusivity. Consider the following approaches:

- Create a safe environment: Prioritize creating a safe and non-judgmental space for open dialogue. Encourage active listening empathy and respect among all participants. Emphasize the importance of treating each other's perspectives with dignity.

- Use "I" statements: When expressing opinions or discussing sensitive topics use "I" statements to communicate how you perceive or feel about the issue. This helps avoid judgment or generalization and focuses the conversation on personal experiences.

- Seek to understand: Instead of jumping to conclusions or making assumptions strive to understand different perspectives. Ask open-ended questions listen actively and show genuine curiosity about others' experiences and viewpoints.

For instance in a multicultural workplace addressing topics such as diversity equity and inclusion can be sensitive. By creating a safe space for conversation encouraging individuals to share their experiences and actively listening to each other's perspectives the organization can foster an inclusive and supportive environment.

In conclusion crisis communication and difficult conversations are inevitable in various aspects of life. By adopting strategies for crisis communication such as crisis response plans and empathetic communication individuals and organizations can navigate challenging situations effectively. Similarly by employing techniques like active listening collaborative problem-solving and constructive feedback difficult conversations can be managed professionally and constructively. These strategies contribute to building stronger relationships fostering growth and resolving conflicts in personal and professional settings.

8

Communication Ethics and Social Responsibility

8.1 Ethical Considerations in Communication:

8.1.1 Honesty and Transparency:

Honesty and transparency are fundamental principles of ethical communication. Communicators have an ethical responsibility to be truthful and provide accurate information. They should avoid misleading or deceptive practices that can harm individuals or organizations. Honesty and transparency build trust and credibility in relationships whether it is between an organization and its employees customers or stakeholders.

For example if a company is faced with a product recall due to safety concerns it is important for the company to communicate the issue honestly and transparently to its customers. This includes admitting the problem explaining the potential risks and outlining the steps the company is taking to address the issue. By being honest and transparent the company demonstrates its commitment to the well-being and trust of its customers.

8.1.2 Privacy and Confidentiality:

Communication professionals often handle sensitive information or have access to confidential data. Respecting privacy and maintaining confidentiality are essential ethical considerations in communication. This includes protecting personal information and ensuring that it is only used for the intended purposes.

For example in the field of healthcare medical professionals have a duty to maintain patient confidentiality. Communication between a doctor and a patient is protected by ethical standards and legal regulations. Patient information should only be shared with authorized individuals and for legitimate reasons. Breaching patient confidentiality can lead to legal consequences and damage the reputation of the healthcare provider.

8.2 Corporate Social Responsibility (CSR) and Communication:
8.2.1 Communicating CSR Initiatives:

Corporate Social Responsibility (CSR) refers to a company's commitment to sustainable practices ethical behavior and contributing to the well-being of society. Effective communication plays a crucial role in promoting and showcasing CSR initiatives to stakeholders including employees customers investors and the general public.

CSR communication should be transparent informative and focused on the impact and benefits of the initiatives. It should highlight how the company's actions align with its values and contribute to the betterment of society or the environment. By effectively communicating CSR initiatives companies can build a positive reputation attract socially conscious consumers and motivate their employees.

For example a clothing company that promotes sustainable manufacturing practices can communicate its CSR initiatives through various channels such as social media press releases and corporate websites. The company may highlight its use of eco-friendly materials fair labor practices and efforts to reduce carbon footprint. By effectively communicating these initiatives the company can differentiate itself from competitors and attract consumers who value sustainability.

8.2.2 Building Trust and Reputation:
Communication ethics and social responsibility are closely tied to reputation management. Companies that prioritize ethical communication and demonstrate social responsibility tend to have a more positive reputation in the eyes of stakeholders. A positive reputation builds trust enhances the company's credibility and can lead to increased customer loyalty and profitability.

Companies should prioritize proactive and honest communication strategies that align with their values and positively impact society. They should engage in open dialogue with stakeholders listen to feedback and address any concerns or criticisms promptly. This helps in building trust and maintaining a positive reputation.

For example when a company is faced with a crisis or controversy such as a product failure or unethical behavior by an employee the way it handles communication can significantly impact its reputation. Openly acknowledging the issue taking responsibility and notifying stakeholders about steps taken to rectify the problem can help rebuild trust. Honest and transparent communication during such challenging times can demonstrate the company's commitment to rectifying mistakes and preventing their recurrence.

In conclusion communication ethics and social responsibility are essential aspects of effective and responsible communication. Ethical considerations such as honesty transparency privacy and confidentiality guide communicators in their interactions with stakeholders. Companies that prioritize corporate social responsibility and effectively communicate their initiatives can build trust enhance reputation and contribute to the betterment of society. By adhering to ethical guidelines and embracing social responsibility organizations can foster positive relationships gain stakeholder support and ensure long-term success.

9

Communication in the Digital Age

Communication in the digital age has been greatly influenced by advancements in technology particularly the rise of social media and the internet. These platforms have provided individuals and organizations with new ways to connect and communicate with others on a global scale. However with these advancements come new challenges and considerations. In this section we will explore two important aspects of communication in the digital age: social media and online presence and cybersecurity and privacy concerns.

9.1 Social Media and Online Presence

9.1.1 Personal Branding and Online Identity

Social media platforms have become a significant tool for personal branding and establishing an online identity. Personal branding refers to the process of creating and managing a distinctive image reputation and persona online. It involves shaping and promoting oneself to align with personal or professional goals.

For example imagine a young professional who wants to establish themselves as an expert in their field. They may use platforms like LinkedIn Twitter or professional blog websites to share their knowledge engage with industry influencers and build a network of like-minded professionals. Through consistent and thoughtful content they can shape their personal brand and be recognized as a credible source in their industry.

On the other hand it's crucial to be mindful of the information one shares online. It's essential to consider the potential impact on one's personal and professional life. Employers and clients often research individuals before making decisions and an online presence can shape their perception. It is important to curate content that positively reflects one's values and goals while maintaining a level of professionalism.

9.1.2 Social Media Etiquette and Best Practices

With the widespread use of social media it is essential to understand and follow social media etiquette and best practices. These guidelines help individuals communicate effectively and respectfully online.

Some key social media etiquettes include:

1. Be mindful of others' privacy: Avoid sharing sensitive and personal information about others without their consent.
2. Engage respectfully: Use polite language and be respectful when engaging in online discussions or debates.

3. Think before you post: Pause and consider the potential impact of your posts before sharing them. Avoid posting anything that may be offensive discriminatory or harmful.

4. Give credit where it's due: When sharing content created by others attribute them appropriately and respect copyright laws.

5. Respond promptly: If someone asks a question or leaves a comment try to respond in a timely manner. This shows engagement and helps build relationships.

Following these best practices helps maintain a positive online presence and fosters meaningful connections with others.

9.2 Cybersecurity and Privacy Concerns

9.2.1 Protecting Personal and Organizational Data

In the digital age safeguarding personal and organizational data has become increasingly important. Cybersecurity refers to the practices and measures taken to protect computer systems networks and information from unauthorized access misuse or damage.

Individuals and organizations must be vigilant in protecting their data against cyber threats such as hacking malware phishing and data breaches. This includes using strong passwords keeping software and systems up to date and encrypting sensitive data. Regularly backing up data and being cautious when sharing personal information online is also crucial.

Moreover organizations should implement security measures

like firewalls intrusion detection systems and employee training programs to educate individuals about potential cybersecurity risks and encourage responsible digital behavior.

9.2.2 Recognizing and Avoiding Online Threats

With the increasing connectivity of the digital world individuals need to be aware of potential online threats and take necessary precautions to avoid them.

Some common online threats include:

1. Phishing: Scammers attempt to obtain sensitive information like passwords or credit card details through deceptive emails or websites.
   Example: A fraudulent email that appears to be from a legitimate bank asking the recipient to verify their account information by clicking on a link.

2. Malware: Malicious software that can infect devices and disrupt or damage data and systems.
   Example: Downloading a file that claims to be a software update but is in fact a virus that compromises the security of the device.

3. Identity Theft: When someone steals another person's personal information to impersonate them or commit fraud.
   Example: An individual's social security number and personal details being stolen leading to unauthorized use of their identity for fraudulent activities.

To avoid these threats individuals should be cautious when sharing personal information online exercise skepticism towards unsolicited emails or messages and utilize antivirus software and firewalls.

In conclusion communication in the digital age has been transformed by social media and online platforms allowing for personal branding and establishing online identities. However it is crucial to be mindful of privacy concerns and adhere to cybersecurity best practices to protect personal and organizational data. By understanding and practicing these principles individuals and organizations can navigate the digital landscape safely and effectively.

Business English phrases

can be useful in various professional contexts:

Meetings and Discussions:

1. Let's kick off the meeting.
2. I'd like to call this meeting to order.
3. Could you please take the minutes?
4. What's on the agenda today?
5. I'd like to propose a new idea.
6. Can we table that for later discussion?
7. Let's circle back to that point.
8. Does anyone have any objections?
9. Can we reach a consensus on this issue?
10. To recap, here are the main points.
11. We need to address this matter urgently.
12. I'd like to open the floor for questions.
13. What are your thoughts on this proposal?
14. Let's brainstorm some solutions.
15. I'm in favor of this approach.
16. I'd like to second that motion.
17. Can you provide some clarification on this?
18. We should explore this further.
19. I'd like to emphasize the importance of this.
20. Let's agree to disagree on this one.

Email and Correspondence:

1. I hope this email finds you well.
2. Please find attached the requested documents.
3. I look forward to your prompt response.
4. Kindly let me know your availability.
5. I appreciate your attention to this matter.
6. Thank you for your cooperation.
7. Please do not hesitate to contact me.
8. I apologize for any inconvenience.
9. Your input is highly valued.
10. I'm writing to follow up on our previous conversation.
11. Here is a summary of our discussion.
12. I'll be out of the office on [date].
13. Please review the attached report.
14. Can you provide an update on the project?
15. I'll get back to you as soon as possible.
16. Let's schedule a conference call.
17. I've cc'd [name] for their input.
18. Your feedback is greatly appreciated.
19. We need to address this issue urgently.
20. I'm copying [name] for their awareness.

Presentations and Reports:

1. I'd like to start by giving an overview.
2. As you can see on the slide,...
3. This graph illustrates our progress.
4. I'd like to highlight some key findings.
5. In conclusion, we have a solid plan.
6. Let's delve into the details.

7. As mentioned earlier,...
8. This data supports our hypothesis.
9. I'll now pass the presentation to [name].
10. Are there any questions at this point?
11. Moving on to the next section,...
12. I'd like to draw your attention to...
13. This chart shows a clear trend.
14. Let's explore this topic further.
15. Our goal is to achieve these objectives.
16. I'd like to share some insights.
17. As outlined in the report,...
18. We can see a positive impact here.
19. To summarize the main points,...
20. Let's move to the Q&A portion.

Negotiations and Agreements:

1. We need to negotiate the terms.
2. Can we find a middle ground?
3. Let's make a counteroffer.
4. I'm confident we can reach an agreement.
5. What are your expectations in this deal?
6. We're looking for a win-win solution.
7. Let's discuss the terms and conditions.
8. I'd like to propose a compromise.
9. We're willing to be flexible on this issue.
10. Can we put this in writing?
11. Let's shake hands on the deal.
12. I'm happy to sign the contract.
13. We've reached a mutually beneficial agreement.
14. It's important to honor our commitments.

15. I'll send you the finalized contract.
16. We'll need to review the fine print.
17. This is a binding agreement.
18. We'll need to adhere to the terms.
19. Let's schedule a follow-up meeting.
20. We'll document all the agreed-upon points.

Networking and Socializing:

1. It's a pleasure to meet you.
2. Can I introduce you to [name]?
3. Let's connect on LinkedIn.
4. I enjoyed our conversation.
5. What line of work are you in?
6. Do you attend many industry events?
7. Let's exchange business cards.
8. Can I get your contact information?
9. Are you familiar with our company?
10. What brings you to this event?
11. I'd love to hear more about your work.
12. Let's grab a coffee sometime.
13. Have you been to this conference before?
14. I'm looking forward to collaborating.
15. What are your professional interests?
16. Let's keep in touch in the future.
17. Can we continue this conversation later?
18. It's been a pleasure meeting you.
19. I hope to see you at future events.
20. Let's explore potential opportunities.

50 Daily life communication tips

1. **Listen Actively:** Pay attention to the speaker and show that you're engaged.
2. **Practice Empathy:** Try to understand and feel what others are experiencing.
3. **Maintain Eye Contact:** It conveys interest and confidence.
4. **Use Open Body Language:** Keep arms uncrossed and stand/sit with an open posture.
5. **Smile:** A warm smile can make you more approachable.
6. **Give Compliments:** Sincere compliments can brighten someone's day.
7. **Mind Your Tone:** Be mindful of your tone of voice; avoid sounding aggressive.
8. **Respect Personal Space:** Give others enough space to feel comfortable.
9. **Be Patient:** Allow others to finish speaking before you respond.
10. **Use Mirroring:** Reflect the speaker's feelings to show you understand.
11. **Avoid Interrupting:** Let people finish their thoughts before you chime in.
12. **Ask Open-Ended Questions:** Encourage deeper conversations.

13. **Use Positive Reinforcement:** Acknowledge and encourage positive behaviors.
14. **Practice Mindfulness:** Stay present in the moment during conversations.
15. **Be Clear and Concise:** Avoid rambling or over-explaining.
16. **Avoid Judging:** Reserve judgment until you fully understand the situation.
17. **Use "I" Statements:** Express your feelings and thoughts without blaming others.
18. **Show Gratitude:** Say "thank you" when appropriate.
19. **Apologize Sincerely:** If you make a mistake, admit it and apologize.
20. **Avoid Gossip:** Refrain from talking negatively about others.
21. **Be a Team Player:** Collaborate and communicate effectively in groups.
22. **Offer Help:** Ask if someone needs assistance when they seem distressed.
23. **Respect Different Opinions:** It's okay to disagree respectfully.
24. **Use Active Voice:** Make your statements more direct.
25. **Stay Calm:** In heated discussions, take a deep breath before responding.
26. **Respect Boundaries:** Don't pry into someone's personal life.
27. **Use Positive Language:** Focus on solutions, not problems.
28. **Avoid Exaggeration:** Stick to the facts when telling a story.
29. **Be Reliable:** Keep your promises and commitments.
30. **Practice Tact:** Deliver tough messages with sensitivity.
31. **Express Appreciation:** Let loved ones know you care about them.

32. **Give Constructive Feedback:** Frame criticism in a helpful manner.
33. **Use Humor Wisely:** Be mindful of the context and your audience.
34. **Avoid Overusing Filler Words:** Like, um, you know, etc.
35. **Use Technology Mindfully:** Don't let screens interfere with face-to-face interactions.
36. **Learn Names:** Address people by their names; it shows respect.
37. **Show Interest:** Ask follow-up questions to demonstrate genuine curiosity.
38. **Adapt to Different Communication Styles:** Adjust your approach based on who you're talking to.
39. **Be Punctual:** Respect others' time by being on time for appointments.
40. **Use Nonverbal Cues:** Nodding or using gestures can show understanding.
41. **Stay Positive:** Focus on solutions rather than dwelling on problems.
42. **Avoid Sarcasm:** It can be easily misunderstood and cause confusion.
43. **Give Credit Where Due:** Acknowledge others' contributions and ideas.
44. **Ask for Feedback:** Seek input on your communication from trusted individuals.
45. **Practice Self-Reflection:** Consider how you can improve your communication.
46. **Limit Distractions:** Put away your phone and other distractions during conversations.
47. **Admit When You Don't Know:** It's okay not to have all the answers.

48. **Avoid Over-Talking:** Don't dominate the conversation; let others speak too.
49. **Be Mindful of Cultural Differences:** Respect diverse backgrounds and customs.
50. **Be Kind:** Above all, treat others with kindness and respect in all your interactions.

50 clothing and grooming tips

Clothing Tips:

1. **Dress for the Occasion:** Choose attire appropriate for your industry and the specific event or meeting.
2. **Invest in Quality Basics:** Start with well-fitting, high-quality essentials like suits, blouses, and dress shoes.
3. **Choose Neutral Colors:** Stick to classic colors like black, gray, navy, and white for a polished look.
4. **Tailor Your Clothing:** Ensure your clothes fit properly; tailoring can make a significant difference.
5. **Accessorize Thoughtfully:** Use accessories like ties, scarves, belts, and jewelry to add a touch of personality.
6. **Maintain a Professional Wardrobe:** Regularly update and refresh your clothing collection.
7. **Wear Wrinkle-Free Clothes:** Invest in wrinkle-resistant fabrics or use a steamer to keep clothes looking sharp.
8. **Button-Up Shirts:** Keep collared shirts buttoned up for a more professional appearance.
9. **Avoid Loud Patterns:** Subtle patterns are generally more appropriate than bold prints.
10. **Wear Closed-Toe Shoes:** Closed-toe shoes are typically more formal and professional.
11. **Choose Classic Styles:** Opt for timeless styles rather than

trendy fashion.
12. **Coordinate Colors:** Ensure your outfit's colors match and complement each other.
13. **Keep Shoes Polished:** Shine your shoes regularly to maintain a professional appearance.
14. **Wear a Belt:** A belt should match your shoes in color and style.
15. **Invest in a Quality Suit:** If applicable to your role, invest in a well-fitted, high-quality suit.
16. **Consider Dress Codes:** Adhere to dress codes in your workplace or industry.
17. **Layer Appropriately:** Wear layers for versatility and comfort in varying temperatures.
18. **Keep Hems Consistent:** Ensure pants and skirt hems are even and sit at the right length.
19. **Use a Garment Bag:** Protect your clothes when traveling with a garment bag.
20. **Avoid Overly Casual Items:** Steer clear of overly casual items like flip-flops, shorts, or ripped jeans.
21. **Check for Dress Code Updates:** Stay informed about changes in your workplace's dress code.
22. **Carry a Professional Bag:** Choose a sleek, well-organized bag for work documents and essentials.
23. **Stay Seasonally Appropriate:** Adjust your wardrobe for different seasons.
24. **Clean Your Clothes:** Regularly launder and dry-clean your clothing.
25. **Wear a Proper-Fitting Bra:** Ensure undergarments provide support and a smooth silhouette.

Grooming Tips:

1. **Maintain Good Hygiene:** Regularly shower, use deodorant, and brush your teeth.
2. **Keep Nails Clean and Trimmed:** Short, clean nails are more professional.
3. **Choose a Suitable Hairstyle:** Opt for a hairstyle that's easy to manage and fits your face shape.
4. **Groom Facial Hair:** Keep facial hair well-groomed and neatly trimmed.
5. **Wear Minimal Perfume/Cologne:** Avoid overpowering scents; opt for subtle fragrances.
6. **Maintain Clear Skin:** Use skincare products to maintain healthy, clear skin.
7. **Regular Haircuts:** Keep your hair trimmed and neat with regular salon visits.
8. **Use Makeup Judiciously:** If you wear makeup, keep it subtle and natural-looking.
9. **Trim and Shape Eyebrows:** Well-groomed eyebrows frame the face.
10. **Stay Sun-Safe:** Protect your skin from the sun to avoid premature aging.
11. **Whiten Teeth:** Consider teeth whitening for a bright smile.
12. **Use Lip Balm:** Keep lips moisturized to prevent chapping.
13. **Watch Your Posture:** Good posture contributes to a confident, professional appearance.
14. **Stay Well-Groomed Overall:** Regularly shave or trim facial and body hair.
15. **Keep Perfume/Cologne Subtle:** Avoid overwhelming scents in close quarters.
16. **Floss Regularly:** Maintain dental hygiene for fresh breath.
17. **Use a Good Razor:** Ensure a clean shave with a quality razor.

18. **Stay Well-Hydrated:** Drink plenty of water for healthy skin.
19. **Clean Glasses/Sunglasses:** Keep eyewear free of smudges and fingerprints.
20. **Wear Sunscreen:** Protect your skin from UV rays to prevent sun damage.
21. **Clean and Organize Accessories:** Keep ties, belts, and other accessories tidy.
22. **Tame Flyaway Hair:** Use hair products to manage unruly hair.
23. **Apply Lotion:** Moisturize your skin to maintain a healthy glow.
24. **Mind Body Odor:** Be aware of body odors and address them promptly.
25. **Practice Daily Self-Care:** Prioritize self-care to look and feel your best.

50 oral communication tips

1. **Speak Clearly:** Enunciate your words and articulate your thoughts clearly.
2. **Moderate Your Pace:** Avoid speaking too quickly; aim for a moderate pace.
3. **Vary Your Tone:** Use a range of tones to convey different emotions and emphasis.
4. **Practice Pausing:** Pause for effect and to allow your audience to absorb information.
5. **Eliminate Fillers:** Minimize the use of "um," "uh," and other filler words.
6. **Control Your Volume:** Adjust your volume to the size of the audience and the setting.
7. **Maintain a Steady Volume:** Avoid speaking too loudly or softly.
8. **Avoid Monotone:** Add inflection to your voice for a more engaging delivery.
9. **Articulate Your Thoughts:** Organize your ideas before speaking to avoid rambling.
10. **Stay on Topic:** Stick to the subject and avoid going off on tangents.
11. **Use Visual Aids:** When appropriate, use visuals to enhance your message.

12. **Make Eye Contact:** Establish a connection with your audience through eye contact.
13. **Read Your Audience:** Adjust your communication based on audience reactions.
14. **Be Confident:** Believe in what you're saying; confidence is contagious.
15. **Gesticulate Appropriately:** Use gestures to emphasize points, but don't overdo it.
16. **Practice Pronunciation:** Work on pronouncing challenging words correctly.
17. **Watch Your Pitch:** Avoid speaking too high or too low; maintain a pleasant pitch.
18. **Be Concise:** Get to the point without unnecessary details.
19. **Use Analogies:** Help your audience relate to your message with relatable comparisons.
20. **Engage with Questions:** Encourage questions to foster interaction.
21. **Mind Your Grammar:** Use proper grammar to convey professionalism.
22. **Use Visual Examples:** Share relevant images or props to illustrate your points.
23. **Practice Vocal Warm-Ups:** Warm up your voice before speaking extensively.
24. **Adapt to Your Audience:** Tailor your language and style to your listeners.
25. **Speak with Passion:** Show enthusiasm for your subject to captivate your audience.
26. **Stay Hydrated:** Drink water to keep your voice clear and hydrated.
27. **Use Positive Language:** Frame messages in a positive and constructive manner.

28. **Avoid Overloading with Information:** Present information in digestible chunks.
29. **Be Sensitive to Timing:** Respect time constraints in conversations and presentations.
30. **Avoid Overuse of Jargon:** Explain technical terms when necessary.
31. **Stay Calm Under Pressure:** Manage nervousness with deep breathing techniques.
32. **Admit If You Don't Know:** It's okay to say, "I don't have the answer right now."
33. **Use Repetition for Emphasis:** Repeat key points to reinforce your message.
34. **Tell Stories:** Stories can make complex topics more relatable.
35. **Practice Active Listening:** Respond thoughtfully to what others say.
36. **Be Open to Feedback:** Welcome constructive criticism to improve.
37. **Use Humor Wisely:** Inject humor when appropriate to lighten the mood.
38. **Be Mindful of Cultural Differences:** Respect diverse cultural norms in communication.
39. **Avoid Interrupting:** Let others finish before responding.
40. **Maintain Professionalism:** Keep emotions in check, especially in professional settings.
41. **Adapt to Different Communication Channels:** Adjust your style for phone, video, and in-person conversations.
42. **Ask for Clarification:** If you don't understand, request further explanation.
43. **Master Transitions:** Use transitional phrases to connect ideas smoothly.

44. **Consider the Environment:** Adjust your volume and pace based on the setting.
45. **Use Nonverbal Cues:** Gestures and facial expressions can enhance your message.
46. **Engage the Audience:** Encourage participation and interaction.
47. **Practice Breath Control:** Deep breaths support your voice and reduce anxiety.
48. **Respect Personal Space:** Maintain appropriate physical distance in conversations.
49. **Be Patient:** Allow others to express themselves fully.
50. **Seek Opportunities for Improvement:** Continuously work on enhancing your oral communication skills.

www.ingramcontent.com/pod-product-compliance
Lightning Source LLC
LaVergne TN
LVHW010606070526
838199LV00063BA/5094